ENGLISH FOXHOUND

A COMPLETE AND RELIABLE HANDBOOK

by Emily Latimer & Suzy Reingold, MFH

RX-124

CONTENTS

History of the English Foxhound 7

The Early English Foxhound in North America 16

Standard of the English Foxhound 20

The Purpose of the English Foxhound 24

Hound Shows and AKC Shows 30
Letters in Connection with Foxhound Registration

Caring for Your Foxhound 41
Grooming · Showing · Nutrition and General Health ·
General Management

Your Puppy's New Home 47
On Arriving Home · The First Night · Other Pets ·
The Early Days · Identification

Feeding Your English Foxhound 59
Factors Affecting Nutritional Needs · Composition and
Role of Food · When to Feed

Training Your English Foxhound 66
Collar and Leash Training · The Come Command · The Sit
Command · The Heel Command · The Stay Command ·
The Down Command · Recall to Heel Command ·
The No Command

Your Healthy English Foxhound 78
Physcial Exam · Healthy Teeth and Gums · Fighting Fleas ·
The Trouble with Ticks · Insects and Other Outdoor Dangers ·
Skin Disorders · Internal Disorders · Worms · Bloat
(Gastric Dilatation) · Vaccinations - Accidents

HISTORY OF THE ENGLISH FOXHOUND

The English Foxhound of today evolved over many years as a refinement of the earliest domesticated hound, a hunting dog. Early man discovered that dogs could assist in bringing down larger and faster game than he could handle alone. From the earliest recorded history, both written and in pictures, there is evidence of dogs being used in hunting. Originally man had to hunt to be able to live, but as civilization progressed, hunting also became a sport. Hounds were held in high esteem, and often fared better than people.

In Great Britain, around the time of the Norman Conquest, two distinct types of hounds began to emerge as a direct result of French importation. Today's English Foxhounds are the descendants of these early hounds. Possibly, these were the Gascon hounds of southwest France, which were quite similar to Bloodhounds. The St. Hubert's breed, or Southern hound, originally hunted deer or hare. This was a larger hound with a good voice but he moved slowly, particularly when following game over rough terrain. Both types of hounds were very heavy-headed with overhanging chops and pendulous dewlaps. Colors varied from mottled pied or liver to nearly black with tan points. Hounds from this era were possessed of great nose and tongue, but were inclined to babble and were lacking drive to a pathetic degree.

The Northern hound was built for speed and possessed many qualities of the Greyhound—and probably even had some Greyhound blood in him. Perhaps due to this cross, these hounds were lacking in nose and cry. Their heads were slender with longer noses and ears. The flews were shallower. Broad backs, gaunt bellies, long joints and small sterns were other general characteristics of this Greyhound-like hunter. The Northern hound came into being later than the Southern hound; gradually the two types merged and were considered staghounds. When the quarry became fox instead is not exactly known. There are mentions of fox hunting as early as an English poem of 1360, and again in a charter given to the Abbot of Peterborough sometime between 1377-1399. But it was not until the middle of the 18th century that fox hunting became widespread. Some sources give a date of 1690 as being the time of the first known pack of hounds kept exclusively for fox hunting.

In the late 1700s and early 1800s the current foxhound was found to be too slow. Breedings were done to develop a lighter and faster hound. Belvoir Furrier was bred at the Belvoir in 1819 and was said to be the best bred hound in the kennel at that time. Even so, he was drafted to Squire Osbaldeston's Quorn Hunt, as he was slightly crooked. There he distinguished himself in the hunt field and was bred from extensively. Somehow, though, during the process of breeding for the desired qualities, the hounds lost some of their voice and nose. At the beginning of the 20th century an attempt was made to add back bone and substance. The old "Peterborough" type hounds were no longer light and racy; they were "Belvoir Tan," standing woodenly on

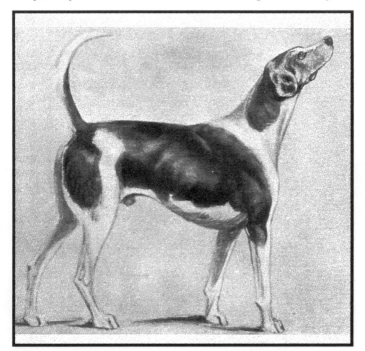

Belvior Furrier, pictured here, was bred in 1819 and was said to be the best bred hound of his time.

The oil painting "Full Cry" by George Vuilefroy portrays a pack of early English Foxhounds. Picture provided by the American Kennel Club.

four legs like bedposts ending in club feet. Wide barrel ribs pushed forward to a shoulder that was placed perpendicular to the ground. These hounds tended to knuckle over and were quite lacking in endurance in the field. "Shorthorn" was the term used to refer to this type of hound. Once again this type was too extreme.

The oil painting "Full Cry," by the 19th-century artist George Vuilefroy of France, depicts four couples of hounds giving chase. Unfortunately there is no information about when this painting was done or even what country it was done in. The landscape could easily be that of England or France. What is so interesting about this painting is that it shows substantial hounds that are not overdone. The hound in the foreground appears to have plenty of bone and muscle and looks as if he could last a full day hunting. The hound to his left, even though his stance is askew, shows no sign of knuckling over.

It is interesting to look at a painting of a hound of the Shorthorn era, Meynell Waverley '09, (whenever a year appears after a hound's name, it refers to the year the hound was entered for hunting and not the year in which he was born) and then to read parts of a description of a foxhound from 1912. In this description it says that there should be symmetry of outline

This painting of Meynell Waverly '09 shows the true hound stature of the day.

with no point in excess. The shoulders should not be overloaded and the center of gravity should be well behind the shoulders. (Look at the knuckling over of this hound. I am not sure where his center of gravity lies!) The back should be level and muscular, not dipping behind the withers or arching over the loin Also for comparison purposes, see a picture of Grafton Pageant from 1901.

In Pageant you see a slight arching over the loin. The next part reads that there should be deep ribs with plenty of heart room. Waverly does not have a particularly deep chest; it barely reaches to the elbow. The back ribs should not be short or appear to tuck up or show weakness through the loin. The hindquarters should show strength and activity. The hind legs and hocks should be placed firm and square underneath to take the weight of the body. Muscles should be strong and carried well down. Again, just looking at this picture, the hindquarters and the forequarters are not that balanced. Waverly was not as extreme as many other hounds of this era. Meynell Wiseacre '11 was quite extreme and almost appeared to be running downhill, yet Wiseacre was awarded Best Single Unentered Dog Hound, and Waverly awarded Champion Dog Hound at the Peterborough show in 1911. In

1924, South Staffordshire Denmark '22 won the Dog Hound Championship at Peterborough. This massive hound had true bedposts for legs, knuckling over at the knee so badly that it is difficult to imagine this hound ever being capable of hunting over rough terrain and lasting for any length of time in the hunt field. Obviously the written description is not what was being produced.

It became evident to breeders of the time that there needed to be a middle ground—that a hound should possess good nose and voice and also be able to move through the fields over the length of a day's hunt. Many Masters of that time felt that this could be accomplished only by outcrossing to other breeds

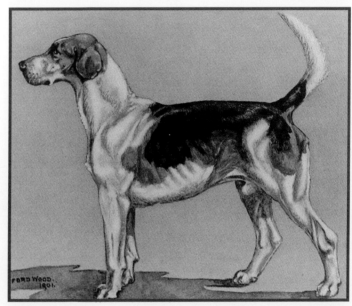

A representation of Grafton Pageant, painted in 1901.

that had the nose, voice and stamina that was desired. Three Masters were determined to breed a better hound with the needed qualities without interspersing these crosses. The Duke of Rutland of the Belvoir, Lord Yarborough of the Brocklesby, and Lord Daresbury of the Limerick stayed strictly to hounds in the English Stud Book. These packs that did not outcross are considered "pure" Old English packs. They carefully chose from blood lines noted for good qualities.

Those Masters that outcrossed wanted to strengthen scenting powers and have hounds that would not break down in the field. It was known that Welsh hounds of French origin produced excellent nose and voice and so were used for this purpose.

These rough-coated Foxhounds from the Duke of Beaufort's pack are sometimes referred to as "Woollies."

These hounds unfortunately also seemed to have a sense of independence that was close to insubordination. The rough coat of the Welsh hounds did not seem to come through in these crosses, but their white color did. (Heavy Welsh crosses did produce rough coats.) Notice here the couple of hounds from the current Duke of Beaufort's pack. These are hounds that are being hunted today, and their picture is included at this point to show the rough coat. The rough-coated hounds are sometimes referred to as "Woollies." Hounds of these crosses were also less uniform in size and shape than the accepted English hound of that era.

Hounds from the Fells of Cumberland and Westmoreland (referred to as Fell Hounds) were also

Mr. Thomas' Flier '26.

Mr. Thomas' Frantic '20.

used in some of these crosses. The Fell Hounds hunted fox in very mountainous terrain. That alone necessitated that they be lighter built, with a hare foot and well-developed hindquarters. Any hound that was overdone and cumbersome would not last very long in that mountainous terrain. The pictures of Mr. Thomas' Flier '26 and Frantic '20 are excellent examples of Fell Hounds. Looking back at Waverley's portrait; the differences are quite obvious. Fell hounds were also brought to America and, along with other crosses, figure in the pedigree of the American Foxhound.

Sir Edward Curre, who hunted the Welsh hills near Chepstow, had been breeding a Welsh cross with clean English lines (but not of Belvoir type). These hounds were able to hunt unassisted with speed and stamina. Sir Edward started developing his pack in the 1890s. The country in which he hunted was quite rough and so he set about breeding a hound that could hunt without much assistance from the huntsman. The hounds needed to have a good nose since the huntsman oftentimes could not follow directly behind them. A good voice was important so the hounds could be heard from a distance, and a light color made them easy to see in the field. Sir Edward

was able to produce such a hound by crossing his rough-coated, excellent-scenting hounds with the light colored Peterborough-type hounds. By about 1925 he had accomplished what he set out to do, and the hounds from these crosses were eligible to be entered into the English Stud Book in 1955. Coming around again, those hounds with Welsh lines are now considered "Peterborough" type.

The Wynnstay hounds, owned by Sir William Watkins-Wynn are considered to be an "old-type" of English Foxhound pack.

Balance in the Foxhound is most important. The traditional purebred foxhound and modern foxhounds continue to be bred with a level topline. However, many of the outcross modern hounds have a slight

A "modern" pack of English Foxhounds owned by the Duke of Beaufort.

arch over the loin, but not as distinctive as that of the American Foxhound. In addition, those who did not outcross and continued to improve the breed produced a more functional hound, eliminating the extreme that fashion had produced. Records have been kept so well through the Masters of Foxhounds Associations (MFHA) that it is easy to trace a hound's pedigree back generation after generation. One can quickly determine if they own a "modern" English Foxhound or an "old" English Foxhound.

Another example of the old type of English Foxhound pack from the Plum Run Hunt in Gettysburg, Pennsylvania.

Here for comparison is one "modern" English pack and two "old" English packs. The first photo is of the Wynnstay hounds owned by Sir William Watkins-Wynn, considered to be "old" English, and the second is of the Duke of Beaufort's pack of "modern" hounds. Notice the wide range of colors in the Beaufort hounds. The third pack is part of the Plum Run Hunt in Gettysburg, Pennsylvania, which is also an "old" English pack.

THE EARLY ENGLISH FOXHOUND IN NORTH AMERICA

The earliest mention of hounds being brought to America occurs in a diary from 1539 written by a member of De Soto's expedition. De Soto brought his army of 600 knights, his priests, his horses, his pack of hounds, and his hogs with him to North America. These hounds were used to hunt Native Americans instead of fox. The first importation of any importance occurred over a hundred years later, in 1650, when Robert Brooke, the first known Master of Foxhounds in America, immigrated to the new colonies, taking with him his entire household, including his pack of hounds. He settled in Maryland, and the descendants of these hounds, known as Brooke hounds, along with other crosses, are the ancestors of today's American Foxhound.

In 1691 there was the first recorded mention of hounds in Virginia. Mike Dixon appeared in court in Northhampton County to answer a complaint that he

The English Foxhound has a long and illustrious history as a hunter in North America, shown here during a parade of hounds at a horse show.

kept a pack of "dogs" that attacked passersby. He was able to convince the judge that his pack of "dogs" destroyed "foxes, wolves and other varmints."

There were many other importations of foxhounds to America, but the next significant importation occurred in 1738 by Lord Fairfax, when it is said that he imported some "fine hounds for the purpose of fox hunting." This pack was said to be the first pack maintained for the benefit of a group of foxhunters rather than for a single owner. They hunted in northern Virginia in territory that is now hunted by the Blue Ridge Hunt, which was organized in 1888.

Lord Fairfax frequently hunted with George Washington, who was said to be an ardent fox hunter and owned his own pack of hounds. It seems that some of

These hounds are hacking to a meet. Hounds must have unrelenting energy and endurance to last all day in the field.

Washington's hounds had the run of Mount Vernon. In particular was a French hound by the name of Vulcan. One day there was a large group of visitors at Mount Vernon and Mrs. Washington had ordered a ham to be prepared for dinner. But alas, when everyone was seated, no ham! Evidently Vulcan had passed through the kitchen and swiped the ham and would not give it up for any reason. Mrs. Washington was not amused, but George thought the incident hilarious. The letters written between Lord Fairfax and George Washington, and the entries in Washington's diary, provide what little is known about foxhunting in that era. It was not until 1890 that the first entries in the Foxhound Stud Book of America were recorded.

The first organized hunt in America was the Gloucester Foxhunting Club that was founded October 29, 1766, in Philadelphia. It continued for 52 years and dissolved in 1818. The earliest established hunt in North America, that is still in existence today, is the Montreal Hunt in Canada, founded in 1826. In the United States, the Piedmont Foxhounds were established in Virginia in 1840 and also still continue today. Another early hunt that still exists today is the Rose

Tree Foxhunting Club in Pennsylvania. The MFHA lists 1859 as the year in which the hunt began, even though there is an oil painting of the Rose Tree Fox Hunting Club that has a date of 1853 on the identification plate. It seems that two gentlemen, Mr. J. Howard Lewis and Mr. George E. Darling, hunted their hounds on foot, as they felt they were too old to ride to hounds. This was the beginning of the Rose Tree, and this painting was done around 1879-1880 of two couples of the Rose Tree hounds. This painting belonged to Theodore Roosevelt, acquired during his years at Harvard, and was given to the American Kennel Club by his daughter. It now hangs in the Roosevelt Room at the AKC along with several other dog paintings that he collected. (There is also a book in the AKC library that is titled *The History of the Rose Tree Fox Hunting Club*.) The standing hounds in the background appear to be the type of hound that were typical of American Foxhounds of that time. The black and tan hound lying down in the foreground looks very much like the Penn-Marydel Hound of today. He is identified as Tuck, who along with Trailer won first prize as best couple at the Delaware County Agricultural and Industrial Society show in 1879. Trailer is the hound standing in the background that is black, tan and

Two couples of Rose Tree Foxhounds, painted in 1879-1880, represent the typical Foxhound of the time. Picture provide by the American Kennel Club.

The English Foxhound is set apart from other breeds by his excellent nose and innate hunting instincts.

white. The two black, tan and white-ticked hounds are Chil, standing, and Hunter, lying to the left of Tuck. Chil won first prize at Philadelphia in 1877, and, with Hunter, won first prize for best couple at the same show. Those two seem a much better pair to be entered as a couple rather than do Tuck and Trailer. The standard also appears on the identification plate of this painting. This standard is almost word for word the English Foxhound Standard of today. It is easy to see why there was confusion and consternation on the part of both judges and breeders. Today the Montreal Hunt is an English pack, the Piedmont Foxhounds an American, Crossbred, English and Penn-Marydel pack, and the Rose Tree a Penn-Marydel pack. It is noteworthy that although English Foxhounds had existed for several centuries in England, and the Masters of Foxhounds Association published stud books, the Foxhound Stud Book only goes back to 1880.

An example of a pack class at a hound show.

STANDARD OF THE ENGLISH FOXHOUND

This is the official standard of the English Foxhound as it was approved by the AKC in 1935.

Head—Should be full size, but by no means heavy. Brow pronounced, but not high or sharp. There should be a good length and breadth, sufficient to give in a dog hound a girth in front of the ears of fully 16 inches. The nose should be long (4 ½ inches) and wide, with open nostrils. Ears set on low and lying close to the cheeks. Most English hounds are "rounded" which means that about 1 ½ inches is taken off the end of the ear. The teeth must meet squarely, either a *pig-mouth* (overshot) or undershot being a disqualification.

Neck—Must be long and clean, without the slightest throatiness, not less than 10 inches from cranium

Opposite: Ch. Plum Run Marathon owned by authors Emily Latimer and Suzy Reingold winning Best of Breed at the 1994 Westminster Dog Show.

First and foremost a hunting dog, the English Foxhound's appearance should reflect utility and competence.

to shoulder. It should taper nicely from shoulders to head, and the upper outline should be slightly convex.

The Shoulders should be long and well clothed with muscle, without being heavy, especially at the points. They must be well sloped, and the true arm between the front and the elbow must be long and muscular, but free from fat or lumber. ***Chest and Back Ribs***—The chest should girth over 31 inches in a 24-inch hound, and the back ribs must be very deep.

Back and Loin—Must both be very muscular, running into each other without any contraction between them. The couples must be wide, even to raggedness, and the topline of the back should be absolutely level, the **Stern** well set on and carried

Shown in a desirable natural stack, the English Foxhound is a hardy athletic dog with stick-straight legs and a weather-resistant, dense coat.

gaily but not in any case curved *over* the back like a squirrel's tail. The end should taper to a point and there should be a fringe of hair below. The ***Hindquarters*** or propellers are required to be very strong, and as endurance is of even greater consequence than speed, straight stifles are preferred to those much bent as in a Greyhound. ***Elbows*** set quite straight and neither turned in nor out are a *sine qua non*. They must be well let down by means of the long true arm above mentioned.

Legs and Feet—Every Master of Foxhounds insists on legs as straight as a post, and as strong; size of bone at the ankle being especially regarded as all important. The desire for straightness had a tendency to produce knuckling-over, which at one time was countenanced, but in recent years this defect has been eradicated by careful breeding and intelligent adjudication, and one sees very little of this trouble in the best modern Foxhounds. The bone cannot be too large, and the feet, in all cases should be round and catlike, with well-developed knuckles and strong horn, which last is of the greatest importance.

Color and Coat—Not regarded as very important, so long as the former is a good "hound color," and the latter is short, dense, hard, and glossy. Hound colors are black, tan and white, or any combination of these three, also the various "pies" compounded of white and the color of the hare and badger, or yellow, or tan. The *Symmetry* of the Foxhound is of the greatest importance, and what is known as "quality" is highly regarded by all good judges.

Scale of Points

Head	5
Neck	10
Shoulders	10
Chest and back ribs	10
Back and loin	15
Hindquarters	10
Elbows	5
Legs and feet	20
Color and coat	5
Stern	5
Symmetry	5
Total	100

Disqualification

Pig-mouth (overshot) or undershot.

The coat of these two dogs illustrate the pied, or almost all-white, color of the English Foxhound.

THE PURPOSE OF THE ENGLISH FOXHOUND

As has been previously discussed, the English Foxhound was developed to hunt fox. As the sport evolved it became important that the hounds assisted the farmers in the control of the fox population to protect farm animals such as chicken and lambs. In the United States only the grey fox is a native. The red fox was originally found in Canada and as far south as Pennsylvania and New Jersey. Some red fox were imported to increase the fox population back in the 19th century. Today, the fox no longer poses a problem to the farmer and the sport is really fox *chasing* instead of fox *hunting*. There are many recorded instances of the fox leading the hounds on a merry chase! Often a fox will run a bit and wait for the hounds

An English Foxhound pack with joint Masters.

A pack animal by nature, the English Foxhound is happiest when in the company of other dogs. This pack of pups wait eagerly for their lunch.

to catch up or even do a bit of hunting himself for mice while the hounds are in pursuit. The term fox hunting is applied to the pursuit of red and grey fox, coyote, and bobcat, depending on location. Coyotes can actually out-fox the hounds by running in relays, with one animal deliberately replacing the original hunted coyote. A successful hunt ends when the fox is accounted for by entering a hole in the ground, called an earth. At one time this was a sport for only the very wealthy, incorporating long-standing traditions. The traditions are still there, but this is now a sport to be enjoyed by people from all walks of life. In North America there are 177 recognized hunts, but only a small percentage are packs comprised of solely English hounds.

Most hunts have members who hunt regularly during the season and can be found helping out with various chores during other times of the year. Many members will even walk out (or raise) puppies for the first months of their lives.

The older hounds must have regular exercise during the off season, and members will often help in this respect. This is called walking out the hounds. Gone are the days when a Master had an entire staff just to look after the hounds. But as said before, the traditions remain. Each hunt has a Master who makes the decisions regarding the hunt. The Huntsman is the person who actually hunts the hounds. He (or she) is assisted by the Whipper-in. The Whipper-in is actually an extension of the Huntsman. He or she rides far out on the flank and is used to help assure that the hounds do the Huntsman's bidding. The mounted field, led by the Field Master (who may also be the

The English Foxhound is a breed that requires plenty of exercise. These hounds are keeping fit during the off season.

Master) follows. Sometimes there will be a second "field" or group of riders called hilltoppers who do not jump. Then there are those who choose to follow the hunt in a four-wheel-drive vehicle. Depending on the hunt country, it is sometimes necessary to have designated people to close gates and to supervise the hilltoppers.

Even the type of hunting clothes worn by the Field is very strictly adhered to. As far back as the 12th century in France it is recorded that special clothes be used for hunting. Grey was the accepted color. Later, in the 14th century, different colors seem to have been worn for hunting different game. Even Chaucer spoke of hunting uniforms. Perhaps the earliest mention of red for hunting comes from Henry IV of France, who wore a red cloak. Green was actually the predominate color worn when stag hunting was prevalent, possibly to conceal the hunters in the forest. From this, different kings and lords had colors to distinguish their followers. Hunts today have different hunt colors that are worn on the lapels of their coats. The hunt staff and Masters usually wear red coats with their hunt colors on the lapels. There is also a practical side to this in that the hunt staff is easily seen in the field in their bright coats.

The Masters of Foxhound Association sets and maintains high sporting standards among its membership. Territories are approved and registered on

The huntsman and hunt staff heading off to the field.

official maps, and disputes of such are settled by the MFHA. Although this may seem strange to have hunt country registered, there is a practical reason for this. If damage should occur to someone's property, then everyone knows who is responsible. Most hunts will also try to help the landowner repair fences and trails through his property. Another practical reason to register country is so that different areas may be hunted on different days and to let members know the area beforehand. If a member is unable to take fences and knows that they will be hunting in Farmer Joe's north field, then that member can decide whether or not he is able to ride from that point.

The hunt staff and masters usually wear red coats with their hunt colors on the lapels, in order to be seen easily in the field.

There are strict rules that must be adhered to for a hunt to be a member of the Association. *The Code of Hunting Practices*, which emphasizes that foxes and coyote must be hunted in their natural state, was recently published by the MFHA. Any other practice that does not give an animal a sporting chance is contrary to the best traditions of the sport and is strictly forbidden. This means that a trapped fox cannot be let loose in front of a pack of hounds. That definitely is not a sporting chance, nor is it in the animal's natural territory. Any hunt that does not follow this code will lose its membership in the Association. A hunt must also have the necessary number of hounds, a minimum of 12 couples (hounds are always counted by twos, hence the word "couple") of registerable hounds if a live hunt, and six couples if a drag hunt. A hunt must also have proper kennel facilities for housing their hounds, and must also have a breeding program to produce their own hounds.

Another wonderful tradition is the Blessing of the Hounds. At the opening meet of the season a priest gives a blessing to the hounds, the foxes and the riders. This is a day for everyone to turn out, and the hounds thoroughly enjoy themselves! Even though they have been out hunting informally prior to the opening meet, they sense that this is something different. While this is supposed to be a solemn occasion (after all, the priest is praying!) the hounds mill around sniffing all the strange people who only

come out once a year. The Huntsman and Whips have their hands full and are more than glad to move off and start the hunting. Usually a "stirrup cup" of port is passed around. After the opening days' meet, most hunts will hold a hunt "breakfast" that can go from the very casual to quite formal. At the end of the season a formal Hunt Ball is held to mark the final day of hunting.

The other really important part of all this is the horse. Most horses used in hunting were bred for that purpose and need to be able to jump different obstacles without hesitation. Also a horse needs to be very sure-footed as the terrain can be varied.

The Blessing of the Hounds is a long-standing ceremony traditionally performed before the opening meet of the hunt season.

PURPOSE OF THE ENGLISH FOXHOUND

In some parts of the country, because of encroaching civilization, there is not enough land to be able to hunt fox. In chasing a fox, the pack can quickly go from one parcel of land to another. The hounds sometimes cross roads and that can become dangerous. Some hunts have gone to drag hunting for these reasons. For a drag hunt, a lure is saturated with fox scent and then dragged across the ground for a good distance. The hounds are then cast and they should pick up this scent and give chase.

Weather conditions can have a great influence on scent. When the air is damp, scent will hold for a long time; conversely, dry, arid conditions cause the scent to dissipate quickly, and hounds can sometimes fail to pick up enough scent to follow. It is important to remember that all hunts (whether they are live or drag) hunt over ground through the courtesy of the landowners. The hounds are trained to ignore all farm animals and other dogs and pursue only the chosen quarry. The chasing of any other wildlife is also not allowed. Hunting season begins in the fall after the crops are harvested and ends before the spring crops are planted.

Although now strictly a recreational sport, the tradition and splendor of the fox hunt have endured throughout the years.

HOUND SHOWS AND AKC SHOWS

In Great Britain, the first hound show was organized by Mr. Thomas Parrington and held at Redcar in 1859 and then established at Peterborough in 1878. For the first six years a Champion Cup was not given and then for three years a Cup was given for the best dog or bitch hound. Since then a Cup has been given for each sex except for the war years of 1915-1919 and again from 1939-1946. There are classes for single unentered hounds, (hounds that have not yet hunted) and for single entered hounds. The same classes are held for couples (two hounds).

This English Foxhound competes in the single unentered hound class. This class is for dogs who have not yet hunted.

Classes are also held for stallion hounds and brood bitches. Hounds are brought into an enclosure on lead by either the Master and Huntsman or the Huntsman and hunt staff. Whoever is actually presenting the hounds will stand in front of them with a biscuit and the assistant stands behind the hounds with lead in hand. After the judge has had an opportunity to observe the hounds in this manner, the leads come off and the biscuits fly! Sometimes an especially gifted Huntsman with "hound appeal" will find himself with hounds from other hunts vying for the biscuit in his hand!

Today there are perhaps six major hound shows held each year in England. All are held during the summer months, and Peterborough remains **the** show.

This huntsman has the complete attention of his hound.

The exact date of the first Puppy Show is unknown, but Will Long, Huntsman from the Badminton Hunt, recorded in his memorandum book in 1840 comments from a puppy show. Although no details are actually given about the first puppy shows, they appear to have started from the giving of prizes to the best puppy walker. Usually the puppies were sent out to local farmers to be walked, and foxhound puppies can often be quite a handful. It was felt that since the walkers were not paid for this that some acknowledgment should be given to encourage that the puppies were well kept. From this, the modern puppy show has developed. Some hunts will have a show just for their own hounds, or several hunts may go together and have a competition between hunts. The format is very similar to regular hound shows except that there are only puppy classes and the atmosphere is much less informal. It should be pointed out that these "puppies" are unentered hounds that are entered to hunt three to four months after the show, and are actually 12–18 months old at the time of the show. Members will usually prepare a buffet or potluck supper after the judging.

Hound shows in North America follow pretty much along the lines of the English shows. In all regular foxhound classes at a recognized show, all entries must have been registered with the MFHA Keeper of the Foxhound Kennel Stud Book or be eligible for such registration. In addition, all fox hound entries must be owned by a recognized or registered hunt or by the Master of such hunt at the time of the show. The classes in North America are similar, but these shows also have pack classes. In the pack classes a hunt must have five couples of hounds to enter. These classes are not held in an enclosure but in an open field. The Huntsman and the Whipper-in bring the hounds in front of the judge to allow them to see the hounds standing together. The hounds are then taken at a trot in a large circle about the size of a football field, coming to stop back in front of the judge. The pack is judged on overall symmetry and on the manner in which the Huntsman controls the hounds. Actually it is more on how the pack responds to the Huntsman.

The hound shows in North America are all held in the Spring, with the Virginia Hound Show and Bryn Mawr in Pennsylvania being the most prestigious. The hound show in Canada is for English Foxhounds only while the five or six in the US have separate

English Foxhounds can also compete as couples, as these two demonstrate at the Canada Hound Show.

classes for English, American and cross-bred Hounds. At Bryn Mawr there are also classes for Basset Hounds, Beagles, and Penn Marydels.

Some hound shows have a horn-blowing contest after the hound judging. Huntsmen and staff are eligible to compete, and the winner is then eligible to compete in the North American Horn Blowing Contest, sponsored by the MFHA. Whippers-in Holloa contests can be another fun part of hound shows.

The American Kennel Club recognizes English Foxhounds, and, therefore, they are eligible to compete in all AKC all-breed shows. Prior to 1909 the AKC did not make a distinction between English and American hounds, they were merely Foxhounds. There are records that exist that show that an American Foxhound was entered in Philadelphia on July 4th, 1876, during America's First Centennial Exposition. When Westminster Kennel Club held its first show in 1877, there were seven American Foxhounds entered. On February 18, 1889, The Brunswick Fur Club (later changed to the Brunswick Foxhound Club) was organized for the purpose of promoting Field Trials for

The biscuits fly as the judge takes advantage of these Foxhounds' enthusiasm to examine their movement and confirmation.

This huntsman finds himself very popular as these Foxhound puppies compete for the remaining biscuits.

American Foxhounds. The first Field Trial was held on November 11, 1889, conducted under rules of the American Kennel Club. No bench show was held at this time. This first trial ran for four days and was won by Joe Forrester, owned by Dr. A.C. Heffinger. The club was so pleased with the results of this first trial that it issued a challenge to other foxhound clubs in the nation. The National Foxhunters' Association held its first field trial on November 20, 1894. At the close of this trial it was voted to have a written standard for the American Foxhound. The first standard for the American Foxhound was written in 1894 by Dr. Heffinger and adopted by the National Fox Hunters Association to more accurately describe an American

At a hound show, the presenter of the hound will stand on front of the dog while his assistant stands behind the dog, holding the lead.

Foxhound. This was not the standard being used to judge foxhounds at AKC events at the time. That standard clearly described an English Foxhound. That standard called for the American Foxhound to be smaller and lighter in muscle and bone. Other points of the standard clearly pointed to a different type of hound. The 1894 standard was printed in the 1896 Westminster catalogue, accompanied by a photo clearly showing English Hounds! It is unknown whether this was just a mistake in printing or whether someone really did not know the difference. Unfortunately the photo is not identified.

In 1903, The Brunswick Fox Hunting Club held its first bench show along with the field trial. This is

Showing their potential, these two youngsters compete in a Foxhound puppy show.

considered the first specialty show for American Foxhounds. Although much support was growing for the leaner, lighter American hound, many good sportsmen preferred the English hound. Mr. A. Henry Higginson from South Lincoln, MA, was a firm believer in the superiority of the English Foxhound. He was challenged to a field trial showdown by Mr. Harry Worchester Smith, who was equally convinced of the superiority of the American hound. The field trial was held during the first two weeks of November, 1905, in Loudon and Fauquier Counties in northern Virginia.

The packs were hunted on alternate weekdays followed by judges on horseback. Many people came from all over the country to witness this showdown. The American pack was declared the winner and Mr. Higginson was so upset that he refused to attend the awards ceremony! This led to the formation of the Masters of Foxhounds Association in 1907, and publication of Volume I of the English Foxhound Stud Book in 1909. Much discussion was carried on at this time between the AKC and breeders of both American and English Foxhounds. There was a great deal of concern that type not be distinguished as field or bench. Some people felt that the current trend was to have one type for field and another for bench instead of two distinct breeds that performed equally well on the bench and in the field. It would be like saying that Bassets and Beagles are the same breed but that one only competed in the field and the other on the bench. (This same discussion was also going on among the English Setter breeders and still continues to this day with several other breeds!) The following two letters from the January 15, 1909 issue of the American Kennel *Gazette* (Vol. 21 No. 1) sum up the controversy.

Letters in Connection With Foxhound Registration

The following letters, which were received by the Stud Book Committee, were omitted from their report published in the minutes of the last meeting. They are included in that report and part of the record.

Brookneal, Va., October 2, 1908

Mr. Marcel A Viti:

Dear Sir: In reply to your letter of the 30th, regarding the proposed division of foxhounds in the AKC Stud Book, I beg to say that this movement will meet with

In the pack classes, a hunt must have five couples of hounds to enter and judging is based upon overall symmetry and the huntsman's ability to control his pack.

This pack of Foxhounds demonstrates their uniform movement and control at a hound show in Virginia.

the majority of sportsmen in America who own and hunt American Foxhounds.

The classes should be separate and distinct, and it is time that the Committee acted upon their own judgment, for upon the action of the Committee will depend the success of the AKC, so far as it pertains to the American Foxhound entries upon the bench shows controlled by this institution.

Thanking you for requesting an expression of my views on the subject, I beg to remain.

Yours very truly,

J.M.Henry

The second letter reads as follows:

Southern Foxhunters Association, October 7,1908

Mr. Marcel A. Viti

Philadelphia

Dear Sir: Replying to yours of 30th ult., it strikes me it would be very advisable to have a division of foxhounds in American and English Classes. My observation is that the owners of the American hounds do not regard the English in the same class in field trials—yet on bench shows the judging seems to be by the English standard. This seems to be the general opinion in the South at least—and owners of American type look with pity on the English Champions in the field—yet they appreciate the tables are turned when they show on the bench where the English standard is the criterion.

To separate them appears to me to be the proper and perhaps the only solution of inducing both to show proper interest.

Yours truly,

C. Floyd Huff

The only opposition to this division seemed to come from the Brunswick Fox Hunting Club. Their letter to the AKC is as follows:

Although usually on horseback, at a hound show the huntsman must follow his pack on foot. This huntsman looks like he's having a hard time keeping up!

Nov. 27, 1908
Mr. Marcel A. Viti
Philadelphia, Pa.

Dear Sir: I have called to the attention of the Brunswick Fox Hunting Club's executive committee your letter stating that "The Stud Book Committee has in consideration the matter of the division of foxhounds, under English Foxhounds and American Foxhounds for registration in the Stud Book."

My Committee believes that an American Foxhound is one which confirms {author's note:conforms? I'm not sure if this is a typographical error or not} in type to the Standard adopted by the Brunswick Foxhound Club, and approved by the National Fox Hunters Association, that type and not blood is the all important factor which determines whether a hound is an American Hound.

Hence if the division in registration is made as you suggest, we believe that any hound, which confirms {Author's note: conforms? Perhaps this writer did not know the difference between confirmation and conformation} to our standard, and whose ancestors are pure bred Foxhounds, should be eligible to registration as an American Foxhound.

The Foxhound standard is printed in the Constitution and By-laws of the Brunswick Foxhound Club, a copy of which is on file with the American Kennel Club.

Very truly,
Bradford S. Turpin
Secretary

Fortunately this was the only dissension, and the AKC went ahead with the division as planned. If Mr. Turpin's viewpoint had prevailed, bloodlines and pedigrees would have been unclear thereafter. After this division the first English Foxhound, as such, was registered with the AKC in 1909. His name was Auditor AKC 129533. He was sired by Bondsman out of Alice and was owned by Clarence Moore of Washington, D.C. Mrs. O. Pryce-Rice of Lianwrda, South Wales, was his breeder. Auditor claims this distinction as he came first in the alphabet of the foxhounds registered after the division. Mr. Moore was the owner of record of 70 of the 80 hounds registered that first year. By looking at their pedigrees we find that all these hounds were brought from England. The first AKC English Foxhound Champion of Record was Langley Drag AKC 132378. Drag was owned by Major W.A. Phipps from Los Angeles. His breeder and date of birth were listed as unknown. In the Stud book his winnings were listed as 1st winners, Los Angeles, 1908, 1st winners, Pasadena 1908. An interesting note from the AKC Stud Book of 1909, under Champions of Record Foxhounds, there are 14 hounds listed. Then there is a subheading (American) with four more hounds listed and then another subheading with (English) listing L. Drag. Both the standard for the English and American Foxhound have changed very little from that time.

Hacking to a meet, these hounds are eager to begin the chase.

The first English Foxhound to win multiple Bests in Show (BIS) was Ch. Mr. Stewart's Cheshire Winslow '81. He was bred by Mrs. Nancy PennSmith Hannum at Mr. Stewart's Cheshire Foxhound in Pennsylvania. He won 25 BIS, 75 Group I placements and multiple other placements. In 1983, Winslow won the most Hound Groups for that year and was awarded the prestigious Quaker Oats award. Three days after that ceremony he also won Group I at Westminster. Winslow retired back to the Plum Run Hunt in Gettsyburg and ended his days enjoying MFH (most favored hound!) status, leading the pack chasing foxes. Several other English Foxhounds have also enjoyed success in the show ring, but his record should stand for generations.

The first English Foxhound to win multiple Bests in Show, this is Ch. Mr. Stewart's Cheshire Winslow '81 bred by Nancy PennSmith Hannum.

CARING FOR YOUR ENGLISH FOXHOUND

GROOMING

A foxhound constantly sheds, similar to a Dalmatian. Their coat also is quite greasy unless bathed frequently and can take on a distinct "hound" odor. Care needs to be taken that a hound is not constantly lying on a hard surface, as unsightly calluses can form at pressure points. When this happens, it results in a loss of hair that generally will never grow back.

If a foxhound is to be shown, there is very little that has to be done to his coat for the ring. A daily brushing with a hound glove takes the dead hair off and helps promote new hair growth. Toenails need to be trimmed weekly and stray hairs around the pads can be

Regular grooming is an excellent way to keep your English Foxhound's coat clean and to detect any coat or skin problems your dog may have.

Your English Foxhound's ears must be kept clean and free of waxy build-up.

neatened. Removal of whiskers is a matter of personal preference. The stern should **never** be blunted, but left in a point. The hair on the underside of the tail must not be trimmed, but may be combed against the grain to make the flag more prominent. This flag of hair is an important feature—it helps the huntsman see the hounds in the field. Sometimes if hounds are going through deep cover the only thing visible is the tip of the stern.

SHOWING

A foxhound should be presented in the ring in hard working condition. You should be able to run your hand over his ribs and feel the individual ribs, but not to the extent of a Saluki. The worst possible thing to do would be to bring an overweight hound into the ring. A hound in good condition should move without rolling.

Opposite: If you accustom your English Foxhound to grooming procedures like nail trimming when he is young, he will come to think of it as a pleasurable experience.

An English Foxhound should be shown on a loose lead and at a moderate pace. The English hounds don't go as fast as their American cousins in the hunt field, and likewise should not race around the show ring. English hounds should be presented in one of two ways. The first is a natural stack with the handler at the end of the lead. This takes some practice and should not be attempted in the ring until you are certain that you have control in this manner. Judges do not appreciate animals moving or jumping on them while they are trying to examine them, and you might end up with disastrous results! The other correct way to way to show an English hound is for the handler to be down on one or both knees holding the dog's head in his right hand and the stern in a curve with his left hand. The stern should never be forced over the back in any way. Unless the handler has a physical disability which makes it difficult for him to get up and down, the handler should not hold the head up with the lead while standing. Most hounds can be kept happy and occupied in the ring with some sort of bait. Foxhounds generally will eat anything that does not eat them first. It is wise to find something that a hound is particularly fond of and save that treat just for the ring.

The English Foxhound should be shown on a loose lead, moving at a moderate pace.

Showing takes a great deal of time and dedication, as well as the ability to control your dog in the ring. As you can see, an English Foxhound can sometimes have a mind of his own!

NUTRITION AND GENERAL HEALTH

Vaccinations are necessary to protect your dog from potentially life-threatening diseases. Your veterinarian can set up an immunization schedule for your English Foxhound.

A good-quality dog food and preventative health care are most important to a healthy hound. Good nutrition is the beginning for a healthy coat. It also goes without saying that all hounds should be seen a least once a year by a veterinarian and receive all immunizations. Many years ago large numbers of

animals were lost due to distemper and other diseases that are now completely preventable. Parasite control is also much easier today with use of different medications to control worms and even fleas and ticks. By keeping your foxhound healthy, he should be with you to the age of 11 or 12. Enjoy!

GENERAL MANAGEMENT

The majority of English Foxhounds are kept in packs and this text will not go into the care and maintenance of a pack. For the person who is caring for a small number of hounds there are just some common sense things to keep in mind.

English Foxhounds have been bred for many generations as pack animals to hunt foxes. Because of their pack nature, some individual hounds do not do as well as household pets as some other breeds. They all require a good deal of exercise for both their physical and mental well being. This means daily long walks or, preferably, jogs. They are not retrievers, so you cannot throw balls for them to bring back to you. A foxhound's instinct is to hunt, but he should never be allowed to hunt on his own. The scent that he is following could take him far afield. The problem would not be that he could not find his way home (a good hound certainly could) rather it would be trespassing, traffic, theft, or other dangers along the way. Foxhounds are very intelligent and learn basic commands quickly; however, they do not generally do well in obedience.

English Foxhounds require a great deal of exercise for both their physical and mental well being.

YOUR PUPPY'S NEW HOME

Before actually collecting your puppy, it is better that you purchase the basic items you will need in advance of the pup's arrival date. This allows you more opportunity to shop around and ensure you have exactly what you want rather than having to buy lesser quality in a hurry.

It is always better to collect the puppy as early in the day as possible. In most instances this will mean that the puppy has a few hours with your family before it is time to retire for his first night's sleep away from his former home.

Before bringing your new English Foxhound puppy home from the breeders, make sure both your family and your household are prepared for your new arrival.

If the breeder is local, then you may not need any form of box to place the puppy in when you bring him home. A member of the family can hold the pup in his lap—duly protected by some towels just in case the puppy becomes car sick! Be sure to advise the breeder at what time you hope to arrive for the puppy, as this will obviously influence the feeding of the pup that morning or afternoon. If you arrive early in the day, then they will likely only give the pup a light breakfast so as to reduce the risk of travel sickness.

PUPPY'S NEW HOME

If the trip will be of a few hours duration, you should take a travel crate with you. The crate will provide your pup with a safe place to lie down and rest during the trip. During the trip, the puppy will no doubt wish to relieve his bowels, so you will have to make a few stops. On a long journey you may need a rest yourself, and can take the opportunity to let the puppy get some fresh air. However, do not let the puppy walk where there may have been a lot of other dogs because he might pick up an infection. Also, if he relieves his bowels at such a time, do not just leave the feces where they were dropped. This is the height of irresponsibility. It has resulted in many public parks and other places actually banning dogs. You can purchase poop-scoops from your pet shop and should have them with you whenever you are taking the dog out where he might foul a public place.

Your journey home should be made as quickly as possible. If it is a hot day, be sure the car interior is amply supplied with fresh air. It should never be too hot or too cold for the puppy. The pup must never be placed where he might be subject to a draft. If the journey requires an overnight stop at a motel, be aware that other guests will not appreciate a puppy crying half the night. You must regard the puppy as a baby and comfort him so he does not cry for long periods. The worst thing you can do is to shout at or smack him. This will mean your relationship is off to a really bad start. You wouldn't smack a baby, and your puppy is still very much just this.

ON ARRIVING HOME

By the time you arrive home the puppy may be very tired, in which case he should be taken to his sleeping area and allowed to rest. Children should not be allowed to interfere with the pup when he is sleeping. If the pup is not tired, he can be allowed to investigate his new home—but always under your close supervision. After a short look around, the puppy will no doubt appreciate a light meal and a drink of water. Do not overfeed him at his first meal because he will be in an excited state and more likely to be sick.

Although it is an obvious temptation, you should not invite friends and neighbors around to see the new arrival until he has had at least 48 hours in which to settle down. Indeed, if you can delay this longer then do so, especially if the puppy is not fully

Opposite: Your English Foxhound puppy will look to you, his owner, for the care and guidance he needs to become a valued family member. An eight-week-old puppy owned by Suzy Reingold and held by Diane Dougherty.

vaccinated. At the very least, the visitors might introduce some local bacteria on their clothing that the puppy is not immune to. This aspect is always a risk when a pup has been moved some distance, so the fewer people the pup meets in the first week or so the better.

Your puppy may be tired from his journey when you first arrive home, so limit visitors and give him plenty of time to rest and relax.

DANGERS IN THE HOME

Your home holds many potential dangers for a little mischievous puppy, so you must think about these in advance and be sure he is protected from them. The more obvious are as follows:

Open Fires. All open fires should be protected by a mesh screen guard so there is no danger of the pup being burned by spitting pieces of coal or wood.

Electrical Wires. Puppies just love chewing on things, so be sure that all electrical appliances are neatly hidden from view and are not left plugged in when not in use. It is not sufficient simply to turn the plug switch to the off position—pull the plug from the socket.

Open Doors. A door would seem a pretty innocuous object, yet with a strong draft it could kill or injure a puppy easily if it is slammed shut. Always ensure there is no risk of this happening. It is most likely during warm weather when you have windows or outside doors open and a sudden gust of wind blows through.

Balconies. If you live in a high-rise building, obviously the pup must be protected from falling. Be sure he cannot get through any railings on your patio, balcony, or deck.

Ponds and Pools. A garden pond or a swimming pool is a very dangerous place for a little puppy to be near. Be sure it is well screened so there is no risk of the pup falling in. It takes barely a minute for a pup—or a child—to drown.

The Kitchen. While many puppies will be kept in the kitchen, at least while they are toddlers and not able to control their bowel movements, this is a room full of danger—especially while you are cooking. When cooking, keep the puppy in a play pen or in another room where he is safely out of harm's way. Alternatively, if you have a carry box or crate, put him in this so he can still see you but is well protected.

Be aware, when using washing machines, that more than one puppy has clambered in and decided to have a nap and received a wash instead! If you leave the washing machine door open and leave the room for any reason, then be sure to check inside the machine before you close the door and switch on.

Puppies love to chew on things, so make sure that all electrical appliances are neatly hidden from view and unplugged when not in use.

Small Children. Toddlers and small children should never be left unsupervised with puppies. In spite of such advice it is amazing just how many people not only do this but also allow children to pull and maul pups. They should be taught from the outset that a puppy is not a plaything to be dragged about the home—and they should be promptly scolded if they disobey.

Children must be shown how to lift a puppy so it is safe. Failure by you to correctly educate your children about dogs could one day result in their getting a very nasty bite or scratch. When a puppy is lifted, his weight must always be supported. To lift the pup, first place your right hand under his chest. Next, secure the pup by using your left hand to hold his neck. Now you can lift him and bring him close to your chest. Never lift a pup by his ears and, while he can be lifted by the scruff of his neck where the fur is loose, there is no reason ever to do this, so don't.

Beyond the dangers already cited you may be able to think of other ones that are specific to your home—steep basement steps or the like. Go around your home and check out all potential problems—you'll be glad you did.

A crate provides your pup with a cozy den to call his own. Make sure to give him plenty of toys to keep him occupied.

THE FIRST NIGHT

The first few nights a puppy spends away from his mother and littermates are quite traumatic for him. He will feel very lonely, maybe cold, and will certainly miss the heartbeat of his siblings when sleeping. To help overcome his loneliness it may help to place a clock next to his bed—one with a loud tick. This will in some way soothe him, as the clock ticks to a rhythm not dissimilar from a heart beat. A cuddly toy may also help in the first few weeks. A dim nightlight may provide some comfort to the puppy, because his eyes will not yet be fully able to see in the dark. The puppy may want to leave his bed for a drink or to relieve himself.

Your English Foxhound puppy may miss the company of his littermates when you first bring his home. Be sure to pay extra attention to him during this lonely time.

If the pup does whimper in the night, there are two things you should not do. One is to get up and chastise him, because he will not understand why you are shouting at him; and the other is to rush to comfort him every time he cries because he will quickly realize that if he wants you to come running all he needs to do is to holler loud enough!

By all means give your puppy some extra attention on his first night, but after this quickly refrain from so doing. The pup will cry for a while but then settle down and go to sleep. Some pups are, of course, worse than others in this respect, so you must use balanced judgment in the matter. Many owners take their pups to bed with them, and there is certainly nothing wrong with this.

The pup will be no trouble in such cases. However, you should only do this if you intend to let this be a permanent arrangement, otherwise it is hardly fair to the puppy. If you have decided to have two puppies, then they will keep each other company and you will have few problems.

OTHER PETS

If you have other pets in the home then the puppy must be introduced to them under careful supervision. Puppies will get on just fine with any other pets—but you must make due allowance for the respective sizes of the pets concerned, and appreciate that your puppy has a rather playful nature. It would be very foolish to leave him with a young rabbit. The pup will want to play and might bite the bunny and get altogether too rough with it. Kittens are more able to defend themselves from overly cheeky pups, who will get a quick scratch if they overstep the mark. The adult cat could obviously give the pup a very bad scratch, though generally cats will jump clear of pups and watch them from a suitable vantage point. Eventually they will meet at ground level where the cat will quickly hiss and box a puppy's ears. The pup will soon learn to respect an adult cat; thereafter they will probably develop into great friends as the pup matures into an adult dog.

HOUSETRAINING

Undoubtedly, the first form of training your puppy will undergo is in respect to his toilet habits. To achieve this you can use either newspaper, or a large litter tray filled with soil or lined with newspaper. A puppy cannot control his bowels until he is a few months old, and not fully until he is an adult. Therefore you must anticipate his needs and be prepared for a few accidents. The prime times a pup will urinate and defecate are shortly after he wakes up from a sleep, shortly after he has eaten, and after he has been playing awhile. He will usually whimper and start searching the room for a suitable place. You must quickly pick him up and place him on the newspaper or in the litter tray. Hold him in position gently but firmly. He might jump out of the box without doing anything on the first one or two occasions, but if you simply repeat the procedure every time you think he wants to relieve himself then eventually he will get the message.

Paper training is one method that is commonly used to housebreak your English Foxhound.

When he does defecate as required, give him plenty of praise, telling him what a good puppy he is. The litter tray or newspaper must, of course, be cleaned or replaced after each use—puppies do not like using a dirty toilet any more than you do. The pup's toilet can be placed near the kitchen door and as he gets older the tray can be placed outside while the door is open. The pup will then start to use it while he is outside. From that time on, it is easy to get the pup to use a given area of the yard.

Many breeders recommend the popular alternative of crate training. Upon bringing the pup home, introduce him to his crate. The open wire crate is the best choice, placed in a restricted, draft-free area of the home. Put the pup's Nylabone® and other favorite toys in the crate along with a wool blanket or other suitable bedding. The puppy's natural cleanliness instincts prohibit him from soiling in the place where he sleeps, his crate. The puppy should be allowed to go in and out of the open crate during the day, but he should sleep in the crate at the night and at other intervals during the day. Whenever the pup is taken out of his crate, he should be brought outside (or to his newspapers) to do his business. Never use the crate as a place of punishment. You will see how quickly your pup takes to his crate, considering it as his own safe haven from the big world around him.

Make sure your English Foxhound puppy has plenty of Nylabones®. They are made of non-toxic polyurethane and help break up plaque on your dog's teeth.

THE EARLY DAYS

You will no doubt be given much advice on how to bring up your puppy. This will come from dog-owning friends, neighbors, and through articles and books you may read on the subject. Some of the advice will be sound, some will be nothing short of rubbish. What you should do above all else is to keep an open mind and let common sense prevail over prejudice and worn-out ideas that have been handed down over the centuries. There is no one way that is superior to all others, no more than there is no one dog that is exactly a replica of another. Each is an individual and must always be regarded as such.

A dog never becomes disobedient, unruly, or a menace to society without the full consent of his owner. Your puppy may have many limitations, but the singular biggest limitation he is confronted with in so many instances is his owner's inability to understand his needs and how to cope with them.

IDENTIFICATION

It is a sad reflection on our society that the number of dogs and cats stolen every year runs into many thousands. To these can be added the number that get lost. If you do not want your cherished pet to be lost or stolen, then you should see that he is carrying a permanent identification number, as well as a temporary tag on his collar.

Permanent markings come in the form of tattoos placed either inside the pup's ear flap, or on the inner side of a pup's upper rear leg. The number given is then recorded with one of the national registration companies. Research laboratories will not purchase dogs carrying numbers as they realize these are clearly someone's pet, and not abandoned animals. As a result, thieves will normally abandon dogs so marked and this at least gives the dog a chance to be taken to the police or the dog pound, when the number can be traced and the dog reunited with its family. The only problem with this method at this time is that there are a number of registration bodies, so it is not always apparent which one the dog is registered with (as you provide the actual number). However, each registra-

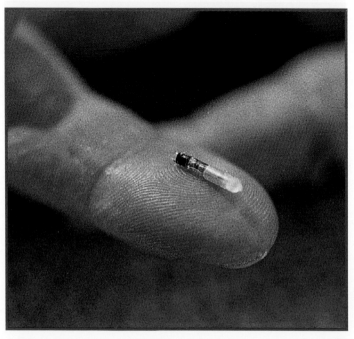

The newest method of identification is the microchip, a computer chip no bigger than a grain of rice that is injected into the dog's skin.

tion body is aware of his competitors and will normally be happy to supply their addresses. Those holding the dog can check out which one you are with. It is not a perfect system, but until such is developed it's the best available.

Another permanent form of identification is the microchip, a computer chip that is no bigger than a grain of rice, that is injected between the dog's shoulder blades. The dog feels no discomfort. The dog also recieves a tag that says he is microchipped. If the dog is lost and picked up by the humane society, they can trace the owner by scanning the microchip. It is the safest form of identification.

A temporary tag takes the form of a metal or plastic disk large enough for you to place the dog's name and your phone number on it—maybe even your address as well. In virtually all places you will be required to obtain a license for your puppy. This may not become applicable until the pup is six months old, but it might apply regardless of his age. Much depends upon the state within a country, or the country itself, so check with your veterinarian if the breeder has not already advised you on this.

It's a big world out there for a little puppy! Make sure your English Foxhound pup is closely supervised to prevent him from become injured or separated from you.

FEEDING YOUR ENGLISH FOXHOUND

Dog owners today are fortunate in that they live in an age when considerable cash has been invested in the study of canine nutritional requirements. This means dog food manufacturers are very concerned about ensuring that their foods are of the best quality. The result of all of their studies, apart from the food itself, is that dog owners are bombarded with advertisements telling them why they must purchase a given brand. The number of products available to you is unlimited, so it is hardly surprising to find that dogs in general suffer from obesity and an excess of vitamins, rather than the reverse. Be sure to feed age-appropriate food—puppy food up to one year of age, adult food thereafter. Generally breeders recommend dry food supplemented by canned, if needed.

FACTORS AFFECTING NUTRITIONAL NEEDS

Activity Level. A dog that lives in a country environment and is able to exercise for long periods of the day will need more food than the same breed of dog living in an apartment and given little exercise.

Quality of the Food. Obviously the quality of food will affect the quantity required by a puppy. If the nutritional content of a food is low then the puppy will need more of it than if a better quality food was fed.

Balance of Nutrients and Vitamins. Feeding a puppy the correct balance of nutrients is not easy because the average person is not able to measure out ratios of one to another, so it is a case of trying to see that nothing is in excess. However, only tests, or your veterinarian, can be the source of reliable advice.

Genetic and Biological Variation. Apart from all of the other considerations, it should be remembered that each puppy is an individual. His genetic make-up will influence not only his physical char-

Show your English Foxhound puppy you care by providing him with a high-quality dog food formulated especially for growth.

acteristics but also his metabolic efficiency. This being so, two pups from the same litter can vary quite a bit in the amount of food they need to perform the same function under the same conditions. If you consider the potential combinations of all of these factors then you will see that pups of a given breed could vary quite a bit in the amount of food they will need. Before discussing feeding quantities it is valuable to know at least a little about the composition of food and its role in the body.

COMPOSITION AND ROLE OF FOOD

The main ingredients of food are protein, fats, and carbohydrates, each of which is needed in relatively large quantities when compared to the other needs of vitamins and minerals. The other vital ingredient of food is, of course, water. Although all foods obviously contain some of the basic ingredients needed for an animal to survive, they do not all contain the ingredients in the needed ratios or type. For example, there are many forms of protein, just as there are many types of carbohydrates. Both of these compounds are found in meat and in vegetable matter—but not all of those that are needed will be in one particular meat or vegetable. Plants, especially, do not contain certain amino acids that are required for the synthesis of certain proteins needed by dogs.

Likewise, vitamins are found in meats and vegetable matter, but vegetables are a richer source of most. Meat contains very little carbohydrates. Some vitamins can be synthesized by the dog, so do not need to be supplied via the food. Dogs are carnivores and this means their digestive tract has evolved to need a high quantity of meat as compared to humans. The digestive system of carnivores is unable to break down the tough cellulose walls of plant matter, but it is easily able to assimilate proteins from meat.

In order to gain its needed vegetable matter in a form that it can cope with, the carnivore eats all of its prey. This includes the partly digested food within the stomach. In commercially prepared foods, the cellulose is broken down by cooking. During this process the vitamin content is either greatly reduced or lost altogether. The manufacturer therefore adds vitamins once the heat process has been completed. This is why commercial foods are so useful as part of a feeding regimen, providing they are of good quality and from a company that has prepared the foods very carefully.

Proteins

These are made from amino acids, of which at least ten are essential if a puppy is to maintain healthy growth. Proteins provide the building blocks for the puppy's body. The richest sources are meat,

This is a healthy treat for your English Foxhound. Its bone-hard structure helps control plaque and when microwaved becomes a rich cracker that your English Foxhound will love. The POPpup™ is fortified with calcium and available in many flavors.

fish and poultry, together with their by-products. The latter will include milk, cheese, yogurt, fishmeal, and eggs. Vegetable matter that has a high protein content includes soy beans, together with numerous corn and other plant extracts that have been dehydrated. The actual protein content needed in the diet will be determined both by the activity level of the dog and his age. The total protein need will also be influenced by the digestibility factor of the food given.

Fats

These serve numerous roles in the puppy's body. They provide insulation against the cold, and help buffer the organs from knocks and general activity shocks. They provide the richest source of energy, and reserves of this, and they are vital in the transport of vitamins and other nutrients, via the blood, to all other organs. Finally, it is the fat content within a diet that gives it palatability. It is important that the fat content of a diet should not be excessive. This is because the high energy content of fats (more than twice that of protein or carbohydrate) will increase the overall energy content of the diet. The puppy will adjust its food intake to that of its energy needs, which are obviously more easily met in a high-energy diet. This will mean that while the fats are providing the energy needs of the puppy, the overall diet may not be providing its protein, vitamin, and mineral needs, so signs of protein deficiency will become apparent. Rich sources of fats are

English Foxhounds require some vegetable matter in their diet. The CarrotBone™ by Nylabone® serves the function of plaque control, satisfies the dog's need to chew, and is nutritious. It is highly recommended as a healthy toy for your English Foxhound.

meat, their byproducts (butter, milk), and vegetable oils, such as safflower, olive, corn or soy bean.

Carbohydrates

These are the principal energy compounds given to puppies and adult dogs. Their inclusion within most commercial brand dog foods is for cost, rather than dietary needs. These compounds are more commonly known as sugars, and they are seen in simple or complex compounds of carbon, hydrogen, and oxygen. One of the simple sugars is called glucose, and it is vital to many metabolic processes. When large chains of glucose are created, they form compound sugars. One

It is fine to give your English Foxhound an occasional treat as long as it does not upset his regular diet.

of these is called glycogen, and it is found in the cells of animals. Another, called starch, is the material that is found in the cells of plants.

Vitamins

These are not foods as such but chemical compounds that assist in all aspects of an animal's life. They help in so many ways that to attempt to describe these effectively would require a chapter in itself. Fruits are a rich source of vitamins, as is the liver of most animals. Many vitamins are unstable and easily destroyed by light, heat, moisture, or rancidity. An excess of vitamins, especially A and D, has been proven to be very harmful.

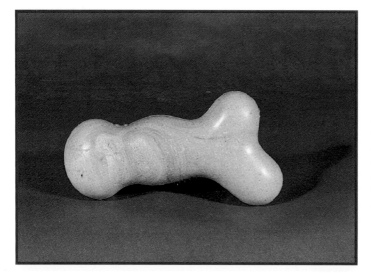

The Galileo™ is the toughest nylon bone ever made. It is flavored to appeal to your English Foxhound and has a relatively soft outer layer. It is a necessary chew device and English Foxhound pacifier.

Provided a puppy is receiving a balanced diet, it is most unlikely there will be a deficiency, whereas hypervitaminosis (an excess of vitamins) has become quite common due to owners and breeders feeding unneeded supplements. The only time you should feed extra vitamins to your puppy is if your veterinarian advises you to.

Minerals

These provide strength to bone and cell tissue, as well as assist in many metabolic processes. Examples are calcium, phosphorous, copper, iron, magnesium, selenium, potassium, zinc, and sodium. The recommended amounts of all minerals in the diet has not been fully established. Calcium and phosphorous are known to be important, especially to puppies. They help in forming strong bone. As with vitamins, a mineral deficiency is most unlikely in pups given a good and varied diet. Again, an excess can create problems—this applying equally to calcium.

Water

This is the most important of all nutrients, as is easily shown by the fact that the adult dog is made up of about 60 percent water, the puppy containing an even higher percentage. Dogs must retain a water balance, which means that the total intake should be balanced by the total output. The intake comes either by direct input (the tap or its equivalent), plus water released when food is oxidized, known as metabolic water (remember that all foods contain the elements hydrogen and oxygen that recombine in the body to create water). A dog without adequate water will lose condition more rapidly than one depleted of food, a fact common to most animal species.

AMOUNT TO FEED

The best way to determine dietary requirements is by observing the puppy's general health and physical appearance. If he is well covered with flesh, shows good bone development and muscle, and is an active alert puppy, then his diet is fine. A puppy will consume about twice as much as an adult (of the same breed). You should ask the breeder of your puppy to show you the amounts fed to their pups and this will be a good starting point.

The puppy should eat his meal in about five to seven minutes. Any leftover food can be discarded or placed into the refrigerator until the next meal (but be sure it is thawed fully if your fridge is very cold).

If the puppy quickly devours its meal and is clearly still hungry, then you are not giving him enough food. If he eats readily but then begins to pick at it, or walks away leaving a quantity, then you are probably giving him too much food. Adjust this at the next meal and you will quickly begin to appreciate what the correct amount is. If, over a number of weeks, the pup starts to look fat, then he is obviously overeating; the reverse is true if he starts to look thin compared with others of the same breed.

WHEN TO FEED

It really does not matter what times of the day the puppy is fed, as long as he receives the needed quantity of food. Puppies from 8 weeks to 12 or 16 weeks need 3 or 4 meals a day. Older puppies and adult dogs should be fed twice a day. What is most important is that the feeding times are reasonably regular. They can be tailored to fit in with your own timetable—for example, 7 a.m. and 6 p.m. The dog will then expect his meals at these times each day. Keeping regular feeding times and feeding set amounts will help you monitor your puppy's or dog's health. If a dog that's normally enthusiastic about mealtimes and eats readily suddenly shows a lack of interest in food, you'll know something's not right.

TRAINING YOUR ENGLISH FOXHOUND

Once your puppy has settled into your home and responds to his name, then you can begin his basic training. Before giving advice on how you should go about doing this, two important points should be made. You should train the puppy in isolation of any potential distractions, and you should keep all lessons very short. It is essential that you have the full attention of your puppy. This is not possible if there are other people about, or televisions and radios on, or other pets in the vicinity. Even when the pup has become a young adult, the maximum time you should allocate to a lesson is about 20 minutes. However, you can give the puppy more than one lesson a day, three being as many as are recommended, each well spaced apart.

Before beginning a lesson, always play a little game with the puppy so he is in an active state of mind and thus more receptive to the matter at hand.

Your English Foxhound must become accustomed to wearing his collar and leash before you begin training exercises.

A pack of hounds paticipating in a parade of hounds at a horse show.

Likewise, always end a lesson with fun-time for the pup, and always—this is most important—end on a high note, praising the puppy. Let the lesson end when the pup has done as you require so he receives lots of fuss. This will really build his confidence.

COLLAR AND LEASH TRAINING

Training a puppy to his collar and leash is very easy. Place a collar on the puppy and, although he will initially try to bite at it, he will soon forget it, the more so if you play with him. You can leave the collar on for a few hours. Some people leave their dogs' collars on all of the time, others only when they are taking the dog out. If it is to be left on, purchase a narrow or round one so it does not mark the fur.

Once the puppy ignores his collar, then you can attach the leash to it and let the puppy pull this along behind it for a few minutes. However, if the pup starts to chew at the leash, simply hold the leash but keep it slack and let the pup go where he wants. The idea is to let him get the feel of the leash, but not get in the habit of chewing it. Repeat this a couple of times a day for two days and the pup will get used to the leash without thinking that it will restrain him—which you will not have attempted to do yet.

Next, you can let the pup understand that the leash will restrict his movements. The first time he realizes this, he will pull and buck or just sit down. Immediately call the pup to you and give him lots of fuss. Never tug on the leash so the puppy is dragged along the floor, as this simply implants a negative thought in his mind.

THE COME COMMAND

Come is the most vital of all commands and especially so for the independently minded dog. To teach the puppy to come, let him reach the end of a long lead, then give the command and his name, gently pulling him toward you at the same time. As soon as he associates the word come with the action of moving toward you, pull only when he does not respond immediately. As he starts to come, move back to make him learn that he must come from a distance as well as when he is close to you. Soon you may be able to practice without a leash, but if he is slow to come or notably disobedient, go to him and pull him toward you, repeating the command. Never scold a dog during this exercise—or any other exercise. Remember the trick is that the puppy must want to come to you. For the very independent dog, hand signals may work better than verbal commands.

THE SIT COMMAND

As with most basic commands, your puppy will learn this one in just a few lessons. You can give the puppy two lessons a day on the sit command but he will make just as much progress with one 15-minute lesson each day. Some trainers will advise you that you should not proceed to other commands until the previous one has been learned really well. However, a bright young pup is quite capable of handling more than one command per lesson, and certainly per day. Indeed, as time progresses, you will be going through each command as a matter of routine before a new one is attempted. This is so the puppy always starts, as well as ends, a lesson on a high note, having successfully completed something.

Call the puppy to you and fuss over him. Place one hand on his hindquarters and the other under his upper chest. Say "Sit" in a pleasant (never harsh) voice. At the same time, push down his rear end and push up under his chest. Now lavish praise on the puppy. Repeat this a few times and your pet will get the idea. Once the puppy is in the sit position you will release your hands. At first he will tend to get up, so immediately repeat the exercise. The lesson will end when the pup is in the sit position. When the puppy understands the command, and does it right away, you can slowly move backwards so that you are a few feet away from him. If he attempts to come to you, simply place him back in the original position and start again. Do not attempt to keep the pup in the sit position for too long. At this age, even a few seconds is a long while and you do not want him to get bored with lessons before he has even begun them.

THE HEEL COMMAND

All dogs should be able to walk nicely on a leash without their owners being involved in a tug-of-war. The heel command will follow leash training. Heel training is best done where you have a wall to one side of you. This will restrict the puppy's lateral movements, so you only have to contend with forward and

Crate training is the quickest and easiest method of housebreaking your English Foxhound.

backward situations. A fence is an alternative, or you can do the lesson in the garage. Again, it is better to do the lesson in private, not on a public sidewalk where there will be many distractions.

With a puppy, there will be no need to use a choke collar as you can be just as effective with a regular one. The leash should be of good length, certainly not too short. You can adjust the space between you, the puppy, and the wall so your pet has only a small amount of room to move sideways. This being so, he will either hang back or pull ahead—the latter is the more desirable state as it indicates a bold pup who is not frightened of you.

Hold the leash in your right hand and pass it through your left. As the puppy moves ahead and strains on the leash, give the leash a quick jerk backwards with your left hand, at the same time saying "Heel." The position you want the pup to be in is such that his chest is level with, or just behind, an imaginary line from your knee. When the puppy is in this position, praise him and begin walking again, and the whole exercise will be repeated. Once the puppy begins to get the message, you can use your left hand to pat the side of your knee so the pup is encouraged to keep close to your side.

It is useful to suddenly do an about-turn when the pup understands the basics. The puppy will now be behind you, so you can pat your knee and say "Heel." As soon as the pup is in the correct position, give him lots of praise. The puppy will now be beginning to associate certain words with certain actions. Whenever he is not in the heel position he will experience displeasure as you jerk the leash, but when he comes alongside you he will receive praise. Given these two options, he will always prefer the latter—assuming he has no other reason to fear you, which would then create a dilemma in his mind.

The Nylabone® Frisbee™ is a must if you want to have fun with your English Foxhound. *The trademark Frisbee is used under license from Mattel Inc. California, USA.*

Once the lesson has been well learned, then you can adjust your pace from a slow walk to a quick one and the puppy will come to adjust. The slow walk is always the more difficult for most puppies, as they are usually anxious to be on the move.

If you have no wall to walk against then things will be a little more difficult because the pup will tend to wander to his left. This means you need to give lateral jerks as well as bring the pup to your side. End the lesson when the pup is walking nicely beside you. Begin the lesson with a few sit commands (which he understands by now), so you're starting with success and praise. If your puppy is nervous on the leash, you should never drag him to your side as you may see so many other people do (who obviously didn't invest in a good book like you did!). If the pup sits down, call him to your side and give lots of praise. The pup must always come to you because he wants to. If he is dragged to your side he will see you doing the

Hunting is just one of the many activities in which the versatile and intelligent English Foxhound can participate. These Hounds check for scent.

dragging—a big negative. When he races ahead he does not see you jerk the leash, so all he knows is that something restricted his movement and, once he was in a given position, you gave him lots of praise. This is using canine psychology to your advantage.

Always try to remember that if a dog must be disciplined, then try not to let him associate the discipline with you. This is not possible in all matters but, where it is, this is definitely to be preferred.

THE STAY COMMAND

This command follows from the sit. Face the puppy and say "Sit." Now step backwards, and as you do, say "Stay." Let the pup remain in the position for only a few seconds before calling him to you and giving lots of praise. Repeat this, but step further back. You do not need to shout at the puppy. Your pet is not deaf; in fact, his hearing is far better than yours. Speak just loudly enough for the pup to hear, yet use a firm voice. You can stretch the word to form a "sta-a-a-y." If the pup gets up and comes to you simply lift him up, place him back in the original position, and start again. As the pup comes to understand the command, you can move further and further back.

The next test is to walk away after placing the pup. This will mean your back is to him, which will tempt him to follow you. Keep an eye over your shoulder, and the minute the pup starts to move, spin around and, using a sterner voice, say either "Sit" or "Stay." If the pup has gotten quite close to you, then, again, return him to the original position.

As the weeks go by you can increase the length of time the pup is left in the stay position—but two to three minutes is quite long enough for a puppy. If your puppy drops into a lying position and is clearly more

Opposite: Who knows how far your puppy can go? This English Foxhound youngster is a pup with potential!

Give your English Foxhound puppies plenty of Nylabones® to play with as a treat after a job well done.

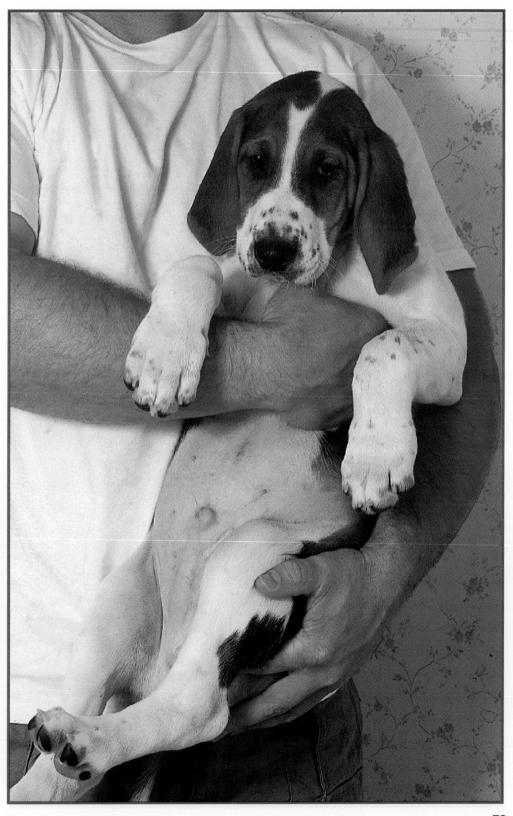

With persistence, practice, and praise, your English Foxhound puppy can become a well-mannered addition to your family.

comfortable, there is nothing wrong with this. Likewise, your pup will want to face the direction in which you walked off. Some trainers will insist that the dog faces the direction he was placed in, regardless of whether you move off on his blind side. I have never believed in this sort of obedience because it has no practical benefit.

THE DOWN COMMAND

From the puppy's viewpoint, the down command can be one of the more difficult ones to accept. This is because the position is one taken up by a submissive dog in a wild pack situation. A timid dog will roll over—a natural gesture of submission. A bolder pup will want to get up, and might back off, not feeling he should have to submit to this command. He will feel that he is under attack from you and about to be punished—which is what would be the position in his natural environment. Once he comes to understand this is not the case, he will accept this unnatural position without any problem.

74

You may notice that some dogs will sit very quickly, but will respond to the down command more slowly— it is their way of saying that they will obey the command, but under protest!

There are two ways to teach this command. One is, in my mind, more intimidating than the other, but it is up to you to decide which one works best for you. The first method is to stand in front of your puppy and bring him to the sit position, with his collar and leash on. Pass the leash under your left foot so that when you pull on it, the result is that the pup's neck is forced downwards. With your free left hand, push the pup's shoulders down while at the same time saying "Down." This is when a bold pup will instantly try to back off and wriggle in full protest. Hold the pup firmly by the shoulders so he stays in the position for a second or two, then tell him what a good dog he is and give him lots of praise. Repeat this only a few times in a lesson because otherwise the puppy will get bored and upset over this command. End with an easy command that brings back the pup's confidence.

The Foxhound is a gregarious dog and thrives on both human and canine companionship.

The second method, and the one I prefer, is done as follows: Stand in front of the pup and then tell him to sit. Now kneel down, which is immediately far less intimidating to the puppy than to have you towering above him. Take each of his front legs and pull them forward, at the same time saying "Down." Release the

legs and quickly apply light pressure on the shoulders with your left hand. Then, as quickly, say "Good boy" and give lots of fuss. Repeat two or three times only. The pup will learn over a few lessons. Remember, this is a very submissive act on the pup's behalf, so there is no need to rush matters.

RECALL TO HEEL COMMAND

Opposite: A well-socialized and properly trained English Foxhound will be welcomed anywhere you go.

When your puppy is coming to the heel position from an off-leash situation—such as if he has been running free—he should do this in the correct manner. He should pass behind you and take up his position and then sit. To teach this command, have the pup in front of you in the sit position with his collar and leash on. Hold the leash in your right hand. Give him the command to heel, and pat your left knee. As the pup starts to move forward, use your right hand to guide him behind you. If need be you can hold his collar and walk the dog around the back of you to the desired position. You will need to repeat this a few times until the dog understands what is wanted.

When he has done this a number of times, you can try it without the collar and leash. If the pup comes up toward your left side, then bring him to the sit position in front of you, hold his collar and walk him around the back of you. He will eventually understand and automatically pass around your back each time. If the dog is already behind you when you recall him, then he should automatically come to your left side, which you will be patting with your hand.

THE NO COMMAND

This is a command that must be obeyed every time without fail. There are no halfway stages, he must be 100-percent reliable. Most delinquent dogs have never been taught this command; included in these are the jumpers, the barkers, and the biters. Were your puppy to approach a poisonous snake or any other potential danger, the no command, coupled with the recall, could save his life. You do not need to give a specific lesson for this command because it will crop up time and again in day-to-day life.

If the puppy is chewing a slipper, you should approach the pup, take hold of the slipper, and say "No" in a stern voice. If he jumps onto the furniture, lift him off and say "No" and place him gently on the floor. You must be consistent in the use of the command and apply it every time he is doing something you do not want him to do.

YOUR HEALTHY ENGLISH FOXHOUND

Dogs, like all other animals, are capable of contracting problems and diseases that, in most cases, are easily avoided by sound husbandry—meaning well-bred and well-cared-for animals are less prone to developing diseases and problems than are carelessly bred and neglected animals. Your knowledge of how to avoid problems is far more valuable than all of the books and advice on how to cure them. Respectively, the only person you should listen to about treatment is your vet. Veterinarians don't have all the answers, but at least they are trained to analyze and treat illnesses, and are aware of the full implications of treatments. This does not mean a few old remedies aren't good standbys when all else fails, but in most cases modern science provides the best treatments for disease.

Opposite: As a responsible English Foxhound owner, you should have a basic understanding of the medical problems that effect the breed.

PHYSICAL EXAMS

Your puppy should receive regular physical examinations or check-ups. These come in two forms. One is obviously performed by your vet, and the other is a day-to-day procedure that should be done by you. Apart from the fact the exam will highlight any problem at an early stage, it is an excellent way of socializing the pup to being handled.

To do the physical exam yourself, start at the head and work your way around the body. You are looking for any sign of lesions, or any indication of parasites on the pup. The most common parasites are fleas and ticks.

the dog's teeth, providing the dog with something safe to chew on will help maintain oral hygeine. Chew devices from Nylabone® keep dogs' teeth clean, but they also provide an excellent resource for entertainment and relief of doggie tensions. Nylabone® products give your dog something to do for an hour or two every day and during that hour or two, your dog will be taking an active part in keeping his teeth and gums healthy…without even realizing it! That's invaluable to your dog, and valuable to you!

Nylabone® provides fun bones, challenging bones, and *safe* bones. It is an owner's responsibility to recognize safe chew toys from dangerous ones. Your dog will chew and devour anything you give him. Dogs must not be permitted to chew on items that they can break. Pieces of broken objects can do internal damage to a dog, besides ripping the dog's mouth. Cheap plastic or rubber toys can cause stoppage in the intestines; such stoppages are operable only if caught immediately.

The most obvious choices, in this case, may be the worst choice. Natural beef bones were not designed for chewing and cannot take too much pressure from the sides. Due to the abrasive nature of these bones, they should be offered most sparingly. Knuckle bones, though once very popular for dogs, can be easily

Nylabone® is the only plastic dog bone made of 100% virgin nylon, specially processed to create a tough, durable, completely safe bone.

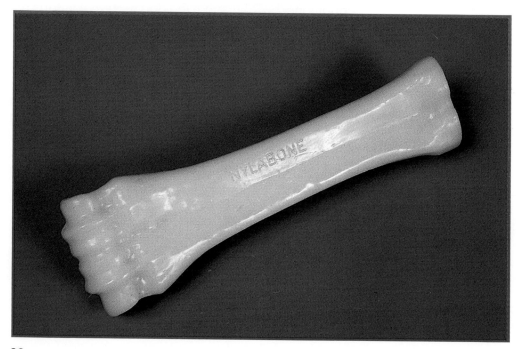

CHICK-N-CHEEZ
CHOOZ
FROM NYLABONE®

NM-106
REGULAR SIZE

TRIPLE PACK

3 For the price of 2

MADE WITH
CHEESE
PROTEIN &
CHICKEN

NO Added Salt or Sugar

Low in Fat

NO Preservatives

Microwaveable

EDIBLE
DIGESTIBLE
HEALTH
CHEW

Foil Packed
For
Sealed-in
Freshness

Chick-n-Cheez Chooz® are completely safe and nutritious health chews made from pure cheese protein, chicken, and fortified with vitamin E. They contain no salt, sugar, plastic, or preservatives and less than 1% fat.

chewed up and eaten by dogs. At the very least, digestion is interrupted; at worst, the dog can choke or suffer from intestinal blockage.

When a dog chews hard on a Nylabone®, little bristle-like projections appear on the surface of the bone. These help to clean the dog's teeth and add to the gum-massaging. Given the chemistry of the nylon, the bristle can pass through the dog's intestinal tract without effect. Since nylon is inert, no micro-organism can grow on it, and it can be washed in soap and water or sterilized in boiling water or in an auto-clave.

For the sake of your dog, his teeth and your own peace of mind, provide your dog with Nylabones®. They have 100 variations from which to choose.

FIGHTING FLEAS

Fleas are very mobile and may be red, black, or brown in color. The adults suck the blood of the host, while the larvae feed on the feces of the adults, which is rich in blood. Flea "dirt" may be seen on the pup as very tiny clusters of blackish specks that look like freshly ground pepper. The eggs of fleas may be laid on the puppy, though they are more commonly laid off the host in a favorable place, such as the bedding. They normally hatch in 4 to 21 days, depending on the temperature, but they can survive for up to 18 months if temperature conditions are not favorable. The larvae are maggot-like and molt a couple of times before forming pupae, which can survive long periods until the temperature, or the vibration of a nearby host, causes them to emerge and jump on a host.

There are a number of effective treatments available, and you should discuss them with your veterinarian, then follow all instructions for the one you choose. Any treatment will involve a product for your puppy or dog and one for the environment, and will require diligence on your part to treat all areas and thoroughly clean your home and yard until the infestation is eradicated.

THE TROUBLE WITH TICKS

Ticks are arthropods of the spider family, which means they have eight legs (though the larvae have six). They bury their headparts into the host and gorge on its blood. They are easily seen as small grain-like creatures sticking out from the skin. They are often picked up when dogs play in fields, but may also arrive in your yard via wild animals—even birds—or stray cats and dogs. Some ticks are species-specific, others are more adaptable and will host on many species.

The cat flea is the most common flea of dogs. It starts feeding soon after it makes contact with the dog.

The deer tick is the most common carrier of Lyme disease. Photo courtesy of Virbac Laboratories, Inc., Fort Worth, Texas.

The most troublesome type of tick is the deer tick, which spreads the deadly Lyme disease that can cripple a dog (or a person). Deer ticks are tiny and very hard to detect. Often, by the time they're big enough to notice, they've been feeding on the dog for a few days—long enough to do their damage. Lyme disease was named for the area of the United States in which it was first detected—Lyme, Connecticut—but has now been diagnosed in almost all parts of the U.S. Your veterinarian can advise you of the danger to your dog(s) in your area, and may suggest your dog be vaccinated for Lyme. Always go over your dog with a fine-toothed flea comb when you come in from walking through any area that may harbor deer ticks, and if your dog is acting unusually sluggish or sore, seek veterinary advice.

Attempts to pull a tick free will invariably leave the headpart in the pup, where it will die and cause an infected wound or abscess. The best way to remove ticks is to dab a strong saline solution, iodine, or alcohol on them. This will numb them, causing them to loosen their hold, at which time they can be removed with forceps. The wound can then be cleaned and covered with an antiseptic ointment. If ticks are common in your area, consult with your vet for a suitable pesticide to be used in kennels, on bedding, and on the puppy or dog.

INSECTS AND OTHER OUTDOOR DANGERS

There are many biting insects, such as mosquitoes, that can cause discomfort to a puppy. Many diseases are transmitted by the males of these species.

A pup can easily get a grass seed or thorn lodged between his pads or in the folds of his ears. These may go unnoticed until an abscess forms.

This is where your daily check of the puppy or dog will do a world of good. If your puppy has been playing in long grass or places where there may be thorns, pine needles, wild animals, or parasites, the check-up is a wise precaution.

SKIN DISORDERS

Apart from problems associated with lesions created by biting pests, a puppy may fall foul to a number of other skin disorders. Examples are ringworm, mange, and eczema. Ringworm is not caused by a worm, but is a fungal infection. It manifests itself as a sore-looking bald circle. If your puppy should have any form of bald patches, let your veterinarian check him over; a microscopic examination can confirm the condition. Many old remedies for ringworm exist, such as iodine, carbolic acid, formalin, and other tinctures, but modern drugs are superior.

After a romp outdoors, be sure to check your English Foxhound's coat for parasites like fleas and ticks.

Fungal infections can be very difficult to treat, and even more difficult to eradicate, because of the spores. These can withstand most treatments, other than burning, which is the best thing to do with bedding once the condition has been confirmed.

Mange is a general term that can be applied to many skin conditions where the hair falls out and a flaky crust develops and falls away.

Often, dogs will scratch themselves, and this invariably is worse than the original condition, for it opens lesions that are then subject to viral, fungal, or parasitic attack. The cause of the problem can be various species of mites. These either live on skin debris and the hair follicles, which they destroy, or they bury themselves just beneath the skin and feed on the tissue. Applying general remedies from pet stores is not recommended because it is essential to identify the type of mange before a specific treatment is effective.

Eczema is another non-specific term applied to many skin disorders. The condition can be brought about in many ways. Sunburn, chemicals, allergies to foods, drugs, pollens, and even stress can all produce a deterioration of the skin and coat. Given the range of causal factors, treatment can be difficult because the problem is one of identification. It is a case of taking each possibility at a time and trying to correctly diagnose the matter. If the cause is of a dietary nature then you must remove one item at a time in order to find out if the dog is allergic to a given food. It could, of course, be the lack of a nutrient that is the problem, so if the condition persists, you should consult your veterinarian.

INTERNAL DISORDERS

It cannot be overstressed that it is very foolish to attempt to diagnose an internal disorder without the advice of a veterinarian. Take a relatively common problem such as diarrhea. It might be caused by nothing more serious than the puppy hogging a lot of food or eating something that it has never previously eaten. Conversely, it could be the first indication of a potentially fatal disease. It's up to your veterinarian to make the correct diagnosis.

The following symptoms, especially if they accompany each other or are progressively added to earlier symptoms, mean you should visit the veterinarian right away:

———————————————

Continual vomiting. All dogs vomit from time to time and this is not necessarily a sign of illness. They will eat grass to induce vomiting. It is a natural cleansing process common to many carnivores. However, continued vomiting is a clear sign of a problem. It may be a blockage in the pup's intestinal tract, it may be induced by worms, or it could be due to any number of diseases.

Diarrhea. This, too, may be nothing more than a temporary condition due to many factors. Even a change of home can induce diarrhea, because this often stresses the pup, and invariably there is some change in the diet. If it persists more than 48 hours then something is amiss. If blood is seen in the feces, waste no time at all in taking the dog to the vet.

Running eyes and/or nose. A pup might have a chill and this will cause the eyes and nose to weep. Again, this should quickly clear up if the puppy is placed in a warm environment and away from any drafts. If it does not, and especially if a mucous discharge is seen, then the pup has an illness that must be diagnosed.

Coughing. Prolonged coughing is a sign of a problem, usually of a respiratory nature.

Wheezing. If the pup has difficulty breathing and makes a wheezing sound when breathing, then something is wrong.

Cries when attempting to defecate or urinate. This might only be a minor problem due to the hard state of the feces, but it could be more serious, especially if the pup cries when urinating.

Cries when touched. Obviously, if you do not handle a puppy with care he might yelp. However, if he cries even when lifted gently, then he has an internal problem that becomes apparent when pressure is applied to a given area of the body. Clearly, this must be diagnosed.

Refuses food. Generally, puppies and dogs are greedy creatures when it comes to feeding time. Some might be more fussy, but none should refuse more than one meal. If they go for a number of hours without showing any interest in their food, then something is not as it should be.

General listlessness. All puppies have their off days when they do not seem their usual cheeky, mischievous selves. If this condition persists for more than two days then there is little doubt of a problem. They may not show any of the signs listed, other than perhaps a reduced interest in their food. There are many diseases that can develop internally without displaying obvious clinical signs. Blood, fecal, and other tests are needed in order to identify the disorder before it reaches an advanced state that may not be treatable.

WORMS

There are many species of worms, and a number of these live in the tissues of dogs and most other animals. Many create no problem at all, so you are not even aware they exist. Others can be tolerated in small levels, but become a major problem if they number more than a few. The most common types seen in dogs are roundworms and tapeworms. While roundworms are the greater problem, tapeworms require an intermediate host so are more easily eradicated.

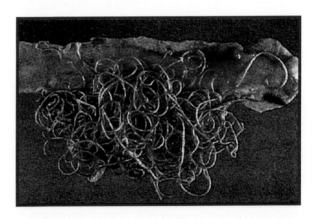

Roundworms are spaghetti-like worms that cause a pot-bellied appearance and dull coat, along with more severe symptoms, such as diarrhea and vomiting. Photo courtesy of Merck AgVet.

Roundworms of the species *Toxocara canis* infest the dog. They may grow to a length of 8 inches (20 cm) and look like strings of spaghetti. The worms feed on the digesting food in the pup's intestines. In chronic cases the puppy will become pot-bellied, have diarrhea, and will vomit. Eventually, he will stop eating, having passed through the stage when he always seems hungry. The worms lay eggs in the puppy and these pass out in his feces. They are then either ingested by the pup, or they are eaten by mice, rats, or beetles. These may then be eaten by the puppy and the life cycle is complete.

Larval worms can migrate to the womb of a pregnant bitch, or to her mammary glands, and this is how they pass to the puppy. The pregnant bitch can be wormed, which will help. The pups can, and should,

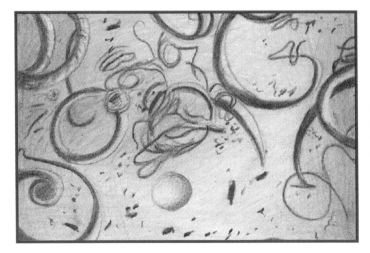

Whipworms are hard to find unless you strain your dog's feces, and this is best left to a veterinarian. Pictured here are adult whipworms.

be wormed when they are about two weeks old. Repeat worming every 10 to 14 days and the parasites should be removed. Worms can be extremely dangerous to young puppies, so you should be sure the pup is wormed as a matter of routine.

Tapeworms can be seen as tiny rice-like eggs sticking to the puppy's or dog's anus. They are less destructive, but still undesirable. The eggs are eaten by mice, fleas, rabbits, and other animals that serve as intermediate hosts. They develop into a larval stage and the host must be eaten by the dog in order to complete the chain. Your vet will supply a suitable remedy if tapeworms are seen or suspected. There are other worms, such as hookworms and whipworms, that are also blood suckers. They will make a pup anemic, and blood might be seen in the feces, which can be examined by the vet to confirm their presence. Cleanliness in all matters is the best preventative measure for all worms.

Heartworm infestation in dogs is passed by mosquitoes but can be prevented by a monthly (or daily) treatment that is given orally. Talk to your vet about the risk of heartworm in your area.

BLOAT (GASTRIC DILATATION)

This condition has proved fatal in many dogs, especially large and deep-chested breeds, such as the Weimaraner and the Great Dane. However, any dog can get bloat. It is caused by swallowing air during exercise, food/water gulping or another strenuous task. As many believe, it is not the result of flatulence. The stomach of an affected dog twists, disallowing food and blood flow and resulting in harmful toxins being released into the bloodstream. Death can easily follow if the condition goes undetected.

The best preventative measure is not to feed large meals or exercise your puppy or dog immediately after he has eaten. Veterinarians recommend feeding three smaller meals per day in an elevated feeding rack, adding water to dry food to prevent gulping, and not offering water during mealtimes.

VACCINATIONS

Every puppy, purebred or mixed breed, should be vaccinated against the major canine diseases. These are distemper, leptospirosis, hepatitis, and canine parvovirus. Your puppy may have received a temporary vaccination against distemper before you purchased him, but be sure to ask the breeder to be sure.

The age at which vaccinations are given can vary, but will usually be when the pup is 8 to 12 weeks old. By this time any protection given to the pup by antibodies received from his mother via her initial milk feeds will be losing their strength.

Rely on your veterinarian for the most effectual vaccination schedule for your English Foxhound puppy.

The puppy's immune system works on the basis that the white blood cells engulf and render harmless

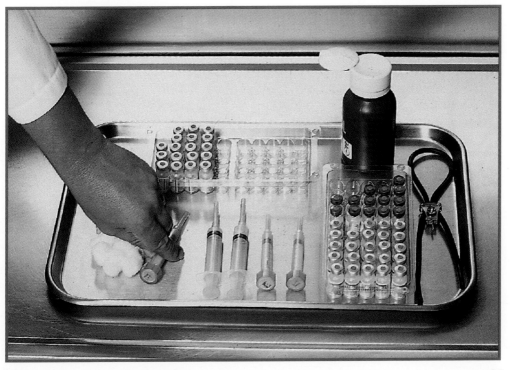

attacking bacteria. However, they must first recognize a potential enemy.

Vaccines are either dead bacteria or they are live, but in very small doses. Either type prompts the pup's defense system to attack them. When a large attack then comes (if it does), the immune system recognizes it and massive numbers of lymphocytes (white blood corpuscles) are mobilized to counter the attack. However, the ability of the cells to recognize these dangerous viruses can diminish over a period of time. It is therefore useful to provide annual reminders about the nature of the enemy. This is done by means of booster injections that keep the immune system on its alert. Immunization is not 100-percent guaranteed to be successful, but is very close. Certainly it is better than giving the puppy no protection.

Dogs are subject to other viral attacks, and if these are of a high-risk factor in your area, then your vet will suggest you have the puppy vaccinated against these as well.

Your puppy or dog should also be vaccinated against the deadly rabies virus. In fact, in many places it is illegal for your dog not to be vaccinated. This is to protect your dog, your family, and the rest of the animal population from this deadly virus that infects the nervous system and causes dementia and death.

ACCIDENTS

All puppies will get their share of bumps and bruises due to the rather energetic way they play. These will usually heal themselves over a few days. Small cuts should be bathed with a suitable disinfectant and then smeared with an antiseptic ointment. If a cut looks more serious, then stem the flow of blood with a towel or makeshift tourniquet and rush the pup to the veterinarian. Never apply so much pressure to the wound that it might restrict the flow of blood to the limb.

In the case of burns you should apply cold water or an ice pack to the surface. If the burn was due to a chemical, then this must be washed away with copious amounts of water. Apply petroleum jelly, or any vegetable oil, to the burn. Trim away the hair if need be. Wrap the dog in a blanket and rush him to the vet. The pup may go into shock, depending on the severity of the burn, and this will result in a lowered blood pressure, which is dangerous and the reason the pup must receive immediate veterinary attention.

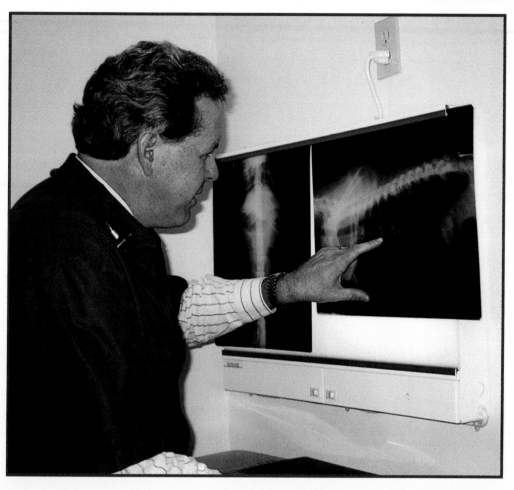

It is a good idea to x-ray the chest and abdomen on any dog hit by a car.

If a broken limb is suspected then try to keep the animal as still as possible. Wrap your pup or dog in a blanket to restrict movement and get him to the veterinarian as soon as possible. Do not move the dog's head so it is tilting backward, as this might result in blood entering the lungs.

Do not let your pup jump up and down from heights, as this can cause considerable shock to the joints. Like all youngsters, puppies do not know when enough is enough, so you must do all their thinking for them.

Provided you apply strict hygiene to all aspects of raising your puppy, and you make daily checks on his physical state, you have done as much as you can to safeguard him during his most vulnerable period. Routine visits to your veterinarian are also recommended, especially while the puppy is under one year of age. The vet may notice something that did not seem important to you.

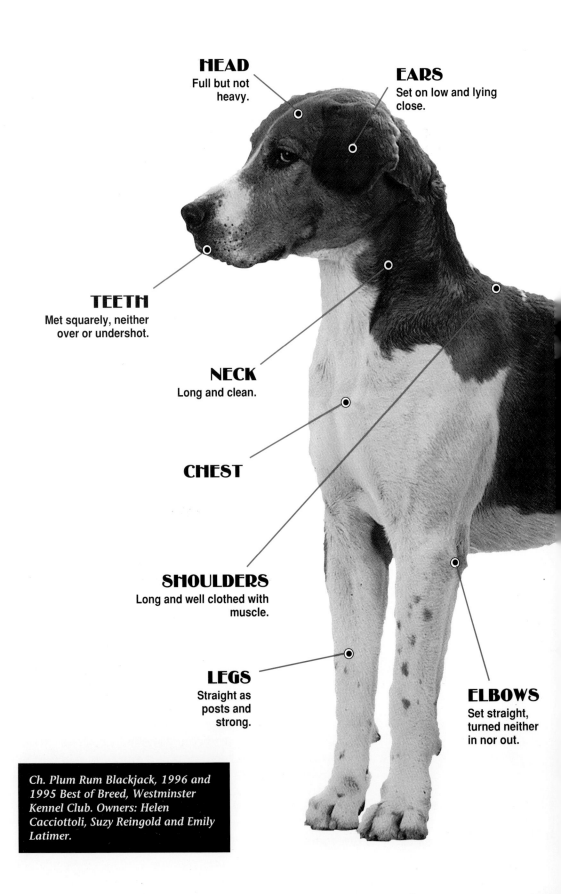

HEAD
Full but not heavy.

EARS
Set on low and lying close.

TEETH
Met squarely, neither over or undershot.

NECK
Long and clean.

CHEST

SHOULDERS
Long and well clothed with muscle.

LEGS
Straight as posts and strong.

ELBOWS
Set straight, turned neither in nor out.

Ch. Plum Rum Blackjack, 1996 and 1995 Best of Breed, Westminster Kennel Club. Owners: Helen Cacciottoli, Suzy Reingold and Emily Latimer.